Love is a Transitive Verb

Love is a Transitive Verb

Poems by
Janice Larson Braun

Published by
The Jackpine Writers' Bloc, Inc.

Published by The Jackpine Writers' Bloc, Inc.
13320 149th Ave, Menahga, MN 56464
sharrick1@wcta.net
www.jackpinewriters.com
Printed in the United States of America
Cover and book design by Tarah L. Wolff
Edited by Sharon Harris

ISBN: 978-1-928690-51-1

Grateful acknowledgment is made to the following
magazines and journals for the previous publication
of these poems:

Talking Stick 27: "Bound," "Two Parts of the Whole"
Talking Stick 28: "Coffee on the Dock," "Just Be"
Talking Stick 29: "Illumination"
Talking Stick 30: "Favors"

Other books by Janice Larson Braun
Finding True North

Table of Contents

Table of Contents

Love is a
Transitive Verb

Consider Love

In the most desolate places
And in the most verdant,
It comes out of nowhere
To the bleak and lifeless landscape,
Tough enough
To withstand drought and heat
Or drenching rains.
In little yellow sunbursts
Love blooms.
In moments of anger in the blackness of despair,
We are driven to pull it out by the roots —
It must be eradicated
If you want a tidy and regulated life.

But if you let it grow and spread,
The pollinators will thank you.

Worthy of Love

A little spruce seedling
Bursts forth
From the orange duff,
Reaching up for the sun,
Stretching down for water.
In its intricate beauty
And profound potential,
It simply is.
And because I believe in innocence,
I bring it buckets of water
When it is dry
And words of love
When the days are long.

We Became Friends

Years ago
When she was tangled
In loneliness
And knotted
With anxiety,
I would hold her
Trembling fear
And tell her she was strong,
      and she would survive this,
      and I loved her.

So yesterday
When she called to report
A warm life
And gentle days—
When instead of saying goodbye
She said, "I love you"—
This time the tears were mine.

Bound

The dog—
Seventy-five pounds
Of sinewy muscle and fuzzy hair—
Slithers into my lap
Belly up
Eyes gazing deeply
Into mine
In a bid for closeness
And a belly rub.
He plants one paw firmly
On my chest—
A lifeline
From his heart
To mine.

Two Parts of the Whole

It was meteoric
The way they came together —
All heat and light —
Impossible not to gaze on
In wonder
And amazement.

And then
They crumbled into pieces
And burned out,
Leaving nothing but ash
As a reminder,
A memory of love.

Winter Solstice

Bleak and stark,
The world
Descends into night.
But the spark
In a stranger's eye,
The warmth
In a beloved voice,
The shelter of an embrace
Sustain us
Day by day
Winter nights.

I plunge into the icy sheets of bed
And coil my body tightly
To kindle whatever flicker
Of heat my body can quicken—
Knowing when I awake,
You will be next to me,
Radiating warmth and security.

Learning to Speak

In the language of love
Slumped shoulders mean
   I need a hug.
A soft kiss means
   We are okay now.
A hand-squeeze on the thigh means
   I'm glad you're here with me.
A thumb rubbing the back of the hand —
   I can't wait to talk about this!
And a steady gaze from across the room?
   You are the one.

Mother Love

Because she knew
I would not drink water,
My mother kept a glass of milk —
Poured and ready for me
At all times in the refrigerator —
My refuge after hard play.
And so it is
When the days are hot and dry,
I ignore my whimpering knees
And carry buckets of water
To all the baby trees —
Tender and thirsty —
Within reach.

A Quiet Word

Sometimes love trickles
When what you really need
Is gushing,
A dam broken wide open.
You can't hold it in your hands
For long,
But love's fluid silkiness
Soothes
And restores balance
In a life that can be dry
And rocky
And parched.

Coffee on the Dock

Romantics teach us to
Seek the truth
And listen to our hearts.
I may not remember the name
Of the woman I met yesterday,
And I may not know *meniscus* from *surface tension*
In the rain gauge,
But I revel in the bounty
Of thundering rain
And the sated peace of the trees.
My heart is true.

I Remember

Expectations
Lapped against the life
I had built for myself.
At first a comfort —
A rhythmic accompaniment
To choices
And seasonal change.

But at some point
They became insistent —
An echoing reminder
Of years drifting by.

The Heat Index

The heat and humidity
Smog
Lies on top of us,
Tail curling around its haunches
Completing the circle,
And purrs—
Content in its crushing
Dominance.
We submit
Paralyzed
And wait for winter.

Waiting for Fall Turnover

Her life is chaotic now —
Filled with dying weeds,
Rough with waves
The wind gusts toss up —
Turbulent
And waiting.

But one morning
She will awaken
To calm serenity
And see with lucid clarity
A new life,
A change in season.

Need

The eyes of the children—
Solemn and expectant—
Haunt me.
The eyes of their mothers,
No longer expectant,
Try to mask fear
With smiles.
I smile back
And modulate my voice
To soothing.
I reach out
And touch an arm.
But the pine needles keep falling
And falling
Until the ground is orange.

We Six

Spending time with old friends
Is like breathing
Crisp Canadian air
As it comes across the lake.
The laughter
The hugs
The gentle smiles
Restore raw hope—
      the strength to stand up
      straight
      under the weight of life
And regenerate
      the cleansing energy
      of love.

Just Be

Earth
Takes a deep breath
And exhales softly
Across the frozen lake.
I stand
At the crest of the hill
And feel her arms
Enfold me,
Her cheek
Resting against the top of my head.
My breathing has slowed,
My heart-center lies open.

Sun Worship

In this dark time of year
The sun is no
Robust male god
Driving his chariot across the sky,
But rather a stately, serene goddess —
A soprano —
Whose liquid voice,
Pure and clear,
Rings across the frozen fields
And seeps into the somber forests.

We stop
And stand in her presence,
Relishing the warm caress
And sweet kiss
Of her song.

Love Blooms

Sometimes
Love is fragile
Like a sweet yellow violet
Tucked up beneath the ferns.
But sometimes
Love is sure and steady
Like the exquisite white daisies
That line the edge
Of the woods.

In Transition

The worrying never stops—
Will she make good choices?
Will she be safe and happy?
After talking to her
My fears soften
And turn to slush—
They seem manageable.
But during the night
They refreeze
And by morning
Look treacherous once again.
I know she will have to
Slip and slide her way through life
As we all do.
And I know
She has a strong core
And a good sense of balance,
But the worrying never stops.

Playing the Bongos

My left hand
Holds my heart's beat—
Strong and steady
And dependable.
My right hand
Frolics lightly
Dancing with joy.
The Beat awakens.

Love Is the Answer

It is one thing
To love chocolate—
To feel its glossy caress
Melting
In your mouth,
The nip of sweetness
On your tongue.
It is quite another thing
To be love in the world—
To melt away fear
With warm compassion
And nip at hatred
With a kiss of peace.

Peace

My spirit longs for rain —
The patter
On the rooftop,
The rivulets
Running down my face,
Down my arms,
Dripping from my fingertips
Until, like the trees,
I simply stand and know.
Even the grumble of distant thunder
Calms me.

God Knows

I have always led
With my heart.
Logic is good
And intellect even better.
But the heart
Listens tenderly
And patiently
And savors truth
As it melts
Like sweet butter
On the tongue.

Illumination

Just as a spider web—
Nearly invisible in the grass—
Blooms radiantly
When bejeweled with morning dew,
So love
Hidden deep in the heart
Glows luminously
When adorned with tears.

Ashes

Until the day he died
The glint in his eye
Sparked joy in me —
A warm glow
Melting all my icy fears
And softening my brittle insecurities.
Now he is gone,
And I am left
Empty
And fragile.
But I rise.

Clarity

I have always been strong-willed —
    dogged
    resolute
    determined
Never interested in conformity.

But love makes us want to bend
In graceful beauty
Like a slender sapling in the woods,
A delicate arch of surrender —
An offering of self.

Layers

Life begins to feel full—
Thousands of faces and names
Stacked up with hundreds
Of book titles and authors,
All topped with one great love.

Sweet memories begin to ooze
And run down the sides,
Mingling and puddling
Where I can taste them—
So many years
Of laughter and tears.

The Yogi

Her heart is pure—
She sees goodness in everyone
And nurtures it
With smiles, kind words, and a gentle touch.
Her fire is warm
The embers bright.
In a world that is too often deceitful,
Pain-filled
And stark,
She believes in hope and justice.
At the end of each session
She sends out peace, compassion
And loving kindness
Into the universe.

Joy

Love released
Is buoyant—
It floats above
All the ripples
In the heart
With heat,
Ever expanding
And free.

Spring

The March sun
Pulses with power —
Seeking out the dark corners,
Making the blues bluer
And greens greener.
It jolts up straight
The spine
That has been bent
Over desks and books
All winter.

April

Longing to see you,
To hear your voice,
I sit at the table
And play solitaire—
A reminder
Not only of your absence
But also of my isolation.
The quiet
Has a monotonous hum—
And Time shifts a shoulder,
Closing its eyes
For a nap.

Fear Revisited

"Forlorn"
Is the word
I'm looking for.
Feeling lost
And alone
But neither.
A solitary loon
Helplessly bobbing
On the rough water,
Waiting
For the call
That will echo
In my heart.

An Ounce of Prevention

Say nothing.
Listen to the chickadees
In the Norway pines,
Watch the waves
Roll into shore,
Retreat
And avoid the hug
That is coming.
You are alone—
You and that awful drug.

So Loved

Love comes in many forms —
Today it is rain
That caresses trees
And lilac bushes
And even rhubarb.
Love gives us what we need
When we need it most,
When we cannot make it
On our own.

The Recipe

The lake is still
In the morning coolness,
Reflecting trees and blue sky.
And the sun lights up
The white boathouse
On the opposite shore.
The birds chirp
With abandon,
And I recognize
The chick-a-dee-dee-dee
And the phoebe calling its name,
Announcing its presence.
An occasional fish jumps,
Leaving circles of ripples.
If we are lucky,
A turtle will poke its head up—
Like a perfect piece of golden toast
Popping up from a toaster.
We belong here,
The dog and I,
In the silken silence
That brings only peace.

Free Love

Those of us
Who grew up in the sixties
With Kahlil Gibran posters
On our dorm walls,
Know that love
Is most powerful
When it is given freely
And returned freely.
Love cannot be trapped
Or held closely
Like a precious stone.
Love must be open
And trusting—
Innocent
And hopeful—
Like the face of a child
Presenting a dandelion bouquet.

Pleas

Just take me with you,
He pleads with big, brown eyes
Gazing into mine,
Hopeful.
I will be good,
The eyes insist:
I will stay right at your side,
I will not pull at the leash
Or bark at deer
Or jump up on neighbors.
And when we return,
I will lie patiently at your feet
And obey your every command.
I will greet you every morning
With face kisses
And snuggle with you
Every night.
Just take me with you.
Please.

Sure Strokes

I love that man
Asleep in the recliner
With a love that pulses
And flows in waves,
Evenly and steadily
Lapping at his feet.

Just watching him
My heart beats
In a gentle cadence
That matches
His quiet snores.

A Duet in Time

Like two voices
Blending
In pure harmony,
The past has begun
To melt into the present:
Sweet childhood memories —
> Sitting hip to hip on the piano bench with my
>> father
> Singing old train-wreck songs,
> Swinging high into the air
> With my mother's sing-song voice
> Reciting, "Oh, what is so rare as a day in June,"
> And speaking Pig Latin
> While eating pine cone soup with my brother.

Old memories
Mingling with and elevating
The monotone
Of each new day.

Favors

On summer mornings
Before the raspberries came in,
My grandma made me
Rhubarb sauce for breakfast.
It was sweet and tart—
A perfect start to the day.
And because I slept with her
In her big bed,
I got to use her chamber pot
Kept under her bed
Until my mother told me
I was big enough
To walk to the outhouse
Like everyone else.
A few years later
Grandma came to stay with us
And slept with me in my bed.
And every morning
I would help her get dressed,
Unrolling her thigh-high nylons
And attaching them
To her garter belt.
One morning she patted my leg
And told me quietly,
"You were always my favorite."

Head vs Heart

The head excels at literary analysis.
It spots
And documents details
Of setting and character
Like "beat-up storefronts"
And "hunched shoulders,"
Noting their effect on plot
And standard themes
Like Loss of Innocence
And Alienation.

But the heart—
The heart feels the pain,
The isolation in a barren world—
And trembles with the fears
And insecurities.
In its search for meaning,
The heart ponders
And lingers over truths
That defy words,
That can only be articulated
With tears.

Winter Love

Walking in the morning snow,
I lift my gaze
And let the flakes
Brush my face.
Suddenly
I am reminded
Of my father's butterfly kisses —
His eyelashes fluttering
Against my cheek
As I sit in his lap
Gently rocking
Until I go limp,
And he carries me
Off to bed.

Peace

for Linda

Sometimes the heart itself
Needs healing.
It needs a band-aid
To hold everything
Safely together
Tenderly
When all the pain
Threatens to explode
And tear it to pieces—
And the love inside
Only hurts.
Sometimes
The heart needs
To breathe.

Shared Trauma

He is so exhausted
That every time he sits down,
He falls asleep.
He has a good heart
And a brilliant mind,
But he is not what my mother called
"A good worker" — a value left over
From the Depression years.
Nonetheless,
If I stand up,
He leaps to his feet
And says, "Eye drop time?"
And leads me patiently
To the line of bottles
On the kitchen counter,
Holds my shoulder,
And meticulously drops in
One drop of twelve for the day.
Then avoiding my injured eye,
He kisses my forehead.
His worry shows
In the deep lines between his eyebrows,
But he laughs and says,
"I think we've got this down."

A Winter's Valentine

Love may not bloom
At thirty below,
But it does shimmer
     and shine
     and glitter
In the sparkling sun.
And on a peaceful morning
It whispers softly
To anyone
Who still sees angels
In the snow.

Finding Humor

Early morning
And my brain on automatic,
I feed the dog
And listen to the morning news.
As I ponder protests
And counter-protests
And wonder at the world,
I make coffee.
Suddenly I realize
I have "dealt out"
Six scoops of coffee
Into the filter that only needs four—
I think.

Too much cribbage,
I conclude,
As I sit in my rocking chair,
Looking out the window
At the frozen lake,
And sip a cup
Of watered-down brew
And pretend this is normal.

Early Spring

Stark
Bleak
And brittle,
All those bare branches
Have survived the winter.
And in the gentle morning rain,
They begin to soften.
Soon
They will be limber
And supple
And sprouting leaves,
Green and glowing —
Laden with grace,
Where all was black
And stoic.

Renascence

Like the steady beating of my heart,
The rain falls,
Softly pattering on the roof.

The trees,
Waking from their winter stupor,
Begin to stretch—
Silent
Amidst all the bird chatter.
Standing with them
On the hilltop
In gentle stillness,
I listen and learn.
We become one.

As I turn to leave
To resume my life,
I whisper, "Happy birthday."

Mothers' Day

Raw fear
Tears at her voice
As she recounts
The horrifying events
That threaten
Her fragile peace of mind —
Her missing and injured cat.
It is the voice of any loving mother
Whose child is distressed
And out of reach.
I understand her terror
And do
What all mothers do —
Speak calmly
And gently
And offer comfort —
Exactly what she will do
When she rescues her cat
And mends
What is broken.

Tigger

I hold him close
And rock him —
A mother's rocking —
To soothe a crying child.

This scrawny, frail cat,
Who took his role
As King of the Jungle
Quite seriously
For over twenty years,
Breathes his final breaths.

When I pass this fragile bundle
To my husband's waiting arms,
He begins to pace —
A father's pacing —
While I continue to rock,
Unable to stop,
Even as the end comes.

Denouement

Without a glance,
Two old hands find each other.
Shoulders and hips
Lock into place —
Two minds
In perfect synchrony,
All the words
Spoken years ago.

Any clashes now
Are simply a motif,
Part of the symphony.
In a moment of clarity
All complications dissolve.

A Mother's Tears

The problem with love
Is that you depend upon it.
It fills you
And makes even the mundane
Sparkle.
But when she departs—
When she flies back
To a life out of hug's reach,
The mundane is even greyer.
The holes left behind
Gape.
And all that remains
Is words.

The Elusive Poem

Lost in a sea of words,
I struggle to surface.
There appears to be no up or down,
No way out.
I can hear it
See glimpses of a pattern
That shifts
When I try to touch it.
It bubbles up around me,
Tickling my skin—
Calling and calling
But never letting me
Grasp it.

The Apple and the Tree

Our roles have changed.
She who never was good
At taking my advice—
Or listening, for that matter—
Now listens
Counsels
And advises
With the voice of authority.
Even from across the country
She directs
With absolute assurance.
I blame her father's genes,
But the truth is
I remember well
All that confidence.

Afloat

There
From across the room
In the midst of that
Gelatinous mass of bodies
And laughing faces,
I see a woman smile at me.
I don't know her,
But that smile,
That gossamer filament
Tossed over the roar,
Connects us,
And I am no longer alone.
So I smile back,
Not yet lost in the sea.

A Moment of Clarity

Gently
It washes over me
Like waves
Lapping on the shore
Easy and comfortable
Bringing no fear
Love is no longer terrifying
I have learned to trust
That it will always be there
And so it comes and goes
Effortlessly
As I sit on the dock
And just be.